CONTENTS

CHAPTER 1

WHAT IS APOLOGETICS?

Always be prepared to make a defense to any one who calls you to
account for the hope that is in you. (I Peter 3:15 RSV)

Before You Read Chapter One

The purpose of *On Guard* is to equip you to give a "reason for the hope that is
in you" (1 Peter 3:15). This is the task of Christian apologetics. As Dr. Craig
explains in the book's opening chapter, apologetics has nothing to do with
apologizing but involves giving a defense of what you believe. Through the study
of apologetics, you will come to appreciate the vital importance of knowing what
you believe and why you believe it.

The tradition of defending Christian beliefs, using the analogy of a formal
court proceeding, is an old one. *Apologia*, the Greek root word of apologetics,
originally referred to "speaking in defense," as in a court of law. Think of this
court analogy when you encounter two other terms we'll use: *argument* and
premise. In logic, as in the courtroom, an argument is a reason offered to prove
a belief. People often use the word "argument" in a way that suggests a conflict.
But when a judge asks a lawyer to present an argument, the judge is not asking
him to fight with anyone. Rather, the argument is a reason that supports the
case.

Formally, an argument consists of one or more statements called premises.
Each premise makes a declaration, such as: "Whatever begins to exist has a

cause." If you can show that all of the premises in your argument are true, then if your argument obeys the rules of logic, they lead inescapably to your proposed conclusion. By using these methods of formal logic, we can provide sound arguments for the truth of Christianity.

The purpose of this study guide is to facilitate understanding, stimulate inquiry, and lead to engaging discussions. Once you have a solid understanding of the material, you can share your knowledge with other believers as well as answer the challenges of skeptics. This study guide will also broaden the scope of your study with supporting information, including exercises, a glossary of some of the terms used, and biographical sketches of individuals mentioned in the text.

The twenty-first century presents both new opportunities and new challenges to our faith. On the one hand, today the case for belief in God and Jesus can be made more powerfully than ever. On the other hand, the movement known as the New Atheism exploits incidents of Islamic terrorism to call all religion into doubt. Skeptics question whether any religion can claim to be true, and cultural elites look down on religious believers who take the Bible seriously. You can address these issues by learning some basic arguments and evidence in support of Christian belief. *On Guard* will provide you with the foundation for a reasonable faith.

We'll begin each chapter of the Study Guide with a short summary of the corresponding chapter in the book. This will be a self-check to make sure that you've got the main points. Then we'll move to reflection and discussion. The reflection section is designed for all readers, even those not in a discussion group. The discussion section is designed for group use. But individual readers will benefit from thinking about the discussion questions as well. If you didn't begin *On Guard* with a study group, you may want to start such a group! Following the discussion section, you'll find a glossary of terms, biographical sketches of the persons mentioned in the chapter, and a list of resources for further study.

Let's get started! Begin by reading chapter one of *On Guard*. After reading, continue with the following summary and reflection and discussion section.

Chapter Summary

Dr. Craig calls us to educate ourselves in the basic defense of Christian belief. He gives three major reasons why apologetics is a vital part of Christian discipleship.

Shaping Culture

We must engage the culture so that Christianity's influence is not diminished. While people who live in a predominately Christian culture may come to faith simply and easily, people raised in a secular culture are skeptical of Christianity. Our major universities, formed centuries ago in the name of Christ, have become hostile toward Christianity. We need to change the perception in our culture that Christians are anti-intellectual.

Strengthening Believers

Knowing what and why you believe will make you a bolder and more confident witness for Christ. It will also help you to persevere in times of doubt and struggle. With your beliefs under attack by the growing secularism in society, you cannot avoid having questions about what you believe. Knowing the answers to common challenges to Christianity and developing a passion for finding new answers will strengthen your faith. It will also make you a more interesting and well-rounded person.

Winning Unbelievers

The ability to win unbelievers improves with apologetic knowledge. You can become a more effective witness for Christ by being equipped to give a reason for the hope within.

Reflection and Discussion

Reflection

Study the sample argument map at the end of chapter one. Make sure you understand how to use it. The map has a "swim lane" format which exhibits the positive argument in the left hand lane labeled "Pro" and the objections that might be raised by an opponent in the right hand lane labeled "Con." The arrows moving back and forth across the lanes trace a possible dialogue between the argument's proponent and opponent. As you progress through *On Guard*, make a habit of reviewing the argument maps that are provided at the end of most chapters. With the major points of the chapter fresh in your memory, the argument map helps assure that you understand how the argument works.

Based on the information in this chapter, take some time to reflect on each of these questions prior to joining your group session. Even if you've never studied apologetics before, you've probably been called upon to explain why you believe in God, or why you are a Christian. Do you think that your explanation at the time was adequate? As you begin this study, try to assess the need for apologetics in your community with these questions:

- What is the attitude toward Christianity in your workplace or school?

- Is it considered politically incorrect to self-identify as a Christian?

- Have you ever been afraid to speak out for Christ because you felt you couldn't answer people's questions?

- Are your beliefs ever challenged? Are you able to defend them if they are?

- Have members of your church identified the need for Christian apologetics?

- What importance is placed on apologetics by friends at church and other Christians?

Discussion

Prior to meeting as a group, review the discussion questions below. You may even want to record your thoughts in a notebook. Be prepared to share your responses with the group. The group leader may choose to assign questions to specific group members or to simply read them aloud for open disucssion.

Have you ever heard people make statements like the following? How do you react when they do? In a group setting, share individual responses to the following statements and then take turns discussing your responses.

- "I'm spiritual, not religious. Why should it matter whether there's a God or not?"

- "The sooner we get rid of this superstitious fantasy of some Big Daddy in the sky, the better. Then, science can take its proper place as the true savior of humanity."

- "Loving kindness is my religion. Just be good to others and don't worry whether there's a God."

- "If there really is a God, he doesn't care how much we suffer."

- "I used to go to church, but when I didn't get anything I prayed for, I realized that there wasn't any God listening."

- "How can you believe that this guy that lived two thousand years ago came back to life from the dead?! Do you expect anyone else to do that? It doesn't make any sense!"

- "Christians are ignorant, bigoted, fascists! They think their religion is the only one that's right!"

> ### ACTIVITY
>
> Save your best responses to each of the skeptics' statements above in a notebook. After completing the last chapter of *On Guard*, you can recall your original answers to judge how much your apologetic ability has improved.

WHAT IS APOLOGETICS? 7

Glossary

Atheism. The belief that God does not exist.

Hare Krishna. Common name for members of the International Society for Krishna Consciousness, a sect of Hinduism.

Pentecost. A biblical event in Acts 2:1-6, where the Christians received the Holy Spirit.

Princeton University. Founded in Princeton, New Jersey, in 1746. One of the eight universities of the Ivy League.

Relativism. A school of philosophy that rejects absolute truths. Moral relativism, for example, rejects absolute moral truths, insisting that morals are determined by social or cultural circumstances.

Secularism. A philosophy which holds that government or other entities should exist separately from religion and/or religious beliefs. It was coined by British writer George Holyoake in 1851.

University of Louvain. (Université Catholique de Louvain) A Belgian university. It is the result of a merger of predecessor institutions, dating back to the fifteenth century. Dr. Craig was a visiting researcher there from 1987–1994.

Skepticism. The philosophical position that judgment should be suspended.

Stanford University. Founded in Stanford, California, in 1891.

University of Porto. (Universidade do Porto) A public university located in Porto, Portugal. Founded in 1911.

Biographical Sketches

Aristotle (384–322 BC). Classical Greek philosopher. He was a student of the Greek philosopher Plato.

Dawkins, Richard (b. 1941). English evolutionary biologist. As the author of *The God Delusion*, Dawkins is an outspoken proponent of atheism.

Harris, Sam (b. 1967). New Atheist author of *The End of Faith* and *Letter to a Christian Nation*. He holds a Ph.D. in neuroscience from the University of California, Los Angeles.

Hitchens, Christopher (b. 1949). English-born American author of *God Is Not Great: How Religion Poisons Everything*. Hitchens' social commentary appears frequently in print and electronic media. His brother, Peter Hitchens, is a Christian. Dr. Craig's debate with Christopher Hitchens at Biola University in 2009 was viewed by over 10,000 people.

Lewis, C. S. (1898–1963). British novelist and academic. Originally an atheist, Lewis became a Christian while a professor at Oxford University. In addition to his works in Christian apologetics, he is known for *The Chronicles of Narnia* and other works of fiction.

Plato (428–347 BC). Classical Greek philosopher. He was a student of the Greek philosopher Socrates.

Socrates (c. 469–399 BC). Greek philosopher. His teachings are known only through his appearance in Plato's dialogues.

Strobel, Lee (b. 1952). American journalist and Christian apologist; former atheist.

Resources

Machen, J. Gresham. "Christianity and Culture." Rep. in *What is Christianity?* Grand Rapids, Mich.: Eerdmans, 1951.

Malik, Charles. "The Other Side of Evangelism." *Christianity Today,* November 7, 1980. Rep. in *The Two Tasks of the Christian Scholar: Redeeming the Soul, Redeeming the Mind.* Ed. Wm. L. Craig and P. Gould. Wheaton, Ill.: Crossway, 2007.

Moreland, J. P. *Love Your God with All Your Mind.* Colorado Springs: Nav Press, 1997.

Wesley, John. "An Address to the Clergy." In *The Works of John Wesley,* 3rd ed. Vol. 10: 480-500. Grand Rapids, Mich.: Baker Book House, 1979.

Wells, David F. *No Place for Truth.* Grand Rapids, Mich.: Wm. B. Eerdmans, 1993.

CHAPTER 2

WHAT DIFFERENCE DOES IT MAKE IF GOD EXISTS?

I considered all that my hands had done and the toil I had spent in doing it, and again, all was vanity and a chasing after wind. (Ecclesiastes 2:11 NRSV)

Before You Read Chapter Two

Do you take God for granted? Dr. Craig begins chapter two with an anecdote about how many people in the former Soviet Union embraced faith in God after living under Marxist atheism. Yet, in America, we have enjoyed religious freedom throughout our history. How do you believe this freedom has affected belief in God?

If you believe in God, have you ever asked yourself why? Is your belief the result of a personal search for answers to life's basic questions? Or have you followed the religious customs of family and friends? As you read chapter two, list the reasons given in the chapter why a belief in God is preferred to a belief in nothing (nihilism).

Chapter Summary

If God does not exist, there is no hope for life beyond the grave. Without God and immortality life is absurd because there is no ultimate meaning, value, or purpose in life. But it is impossible to live consistently and happily with such a worldview. Atheists thus live in denial of their own worldview, and their position becomes impossible to sustain.

By contrast, biblical Christianity succeeds in providing what atheism cannot. God provides the foundation for the meaning, value, and purpose of life. Dr. Craig shares his own personal testimony of his journey from despair to life in Christ.

Reflection and Discussion

Reflection

Before attempting to answer the following thoughts, make sure that you've grasped the basic ideas presented in this chapter. Take a few moments to look over the chapter again and summarize the reasons given for why life is absurd if God does not exist. If you have never considered the difference that God makes, now is the time. It's an issue too important to ignore.

Next, list the potential consequences of God's not existing, both the reasons given in the chapter and any others that might have occurred to you. Then list the consequences of God's existing.

In a group setting, compare the items on each other's lists, and then ask volunteers to share what they thought were the most compelling ideas presented.

Discussion

Prior to meeting as a group, review the discussion questions below. You may even want to record your thoughts in a notebook. Be prepared to share your responses with the group. The group leader may choose to assign questions to specific group members or to simply read them aloud for open disucssion.

 ◆ What signs of cultural deterioration do you see as a result of denial of God's existence?

- What are the benefits of knowing that your life has meaning? How does it affect your attitude toward other people?

- If atheists, such as Sartre and Russell, believe that moral values and duties aren't real, then how do they arrive at the values that they want to pretend are real?

- Imagine a world where *everyone* believed that moral values and duties aren't real, but are just subjective illusions. How would it affect:

  > Our legal and judicial systems?
  > Countries involved in warfare?
  > Our social relationships?
  > World business and commerce?

For Further Discussion

If time permits, you may discuss these questions in your group, or consider them later during personal study.

- Sartre produced most of his philosophic writing during and immediately after World War II. What effect might this have had on his view of mankind, the world, and the question of God's existence?

- Dr. Craig's personal journey to faith in Jesus Christ began by understanding his mortality—knowing that he would die some day. Consider two of the men mentioned in the chapter—Duvalier and Mengele. Both of them were mass murderers. They destroyed the lives of others without any fear of retaliation. Do you think such men allow themselves to be aware of their own mortality?

- Would Duvalier and Mengele consider themselves to be superior beings to the people they killed? If God did not exist, would it be possible to accord equal value to all human lives?

Glossary

DNA. Deoxyribonucleic acid; the basic "building block" of proteins and other components of living cells.

Existentialism. A school of philosophy which, among other things, focuses on the conditions of an individual's existence. Danish philosopher Søren Kierkegaard is considered the founder of Existentialism. Though Kierkegaard was a Christian, many of the later existentialist philosophers—such as Nietzsche, Sartre, and Camus—have been atheists.

Nihilism. A philosophical doctrine which argues that life is without meaning, value, or purpose.

Vivisection. Surgical dissection of a living specimen to view the functions of its internal organs.

Biographical Sketches

Camus, Albert (1913–1960). French existentialist novelist and dramatist.

Dawkins, Richard (b. 1941). English evolutionary biologist. As the author of *The God Delusion*, Dawkins is an outspoken proponent of atheism.

Duvalier, François "Papa Doc" (1907–1971). President of Haiti from 1957–1971. His regime was responsible for as many as 30,000 deaths.

Marcos, Ferdinand (1917–1989). President of the Philippines from 1965–1986. He is infamous for his human rights violations and economic corruption.

Mengele, Dr. Josef (1911–1979). German physician. He performed human experiments on Jews and other prisoners at the Nazi concentration camp Auschwitz-Birkenau.

Nietzsche, Friedrich (1844–1900). German philosopher. As an atheist, his statement "God is dead" appears *The Gay Science* and other personal works. Nietzsche also attacked traditional Christian morality and its concept of good and evil, asserting that morals should instead be distinguished between what is 'life-affirming' and 'life-denying.'

Pascal, Blaise (1623–1662). French mathematician and philosopher. He is best known for Pascal's Wager, which asserts that even though God's existence cannot be proven through arguments, a person should wager that God exists, because in so believing one has everything to gain and nothing to lose.

Russell, Bertrand (1872–1970). English mathematician and philosopher. Author of *Why I Am Not a Christian*.

Sartre, Jean-Paul (1905–1980). French existentialist philosopher. Author of *Being and Nothingness* and other works.

Schaeffer, Francis (1912–1984). Christian theologian and pastor. He was the founder of the L'Abri community in Switzerland. Author of *The God Who Is There* and other works.

Tillich, Paul (1886–1965). German Lutheran theologian. Tillich used his "method of correlation" as a means of applying existentialist philosophy to Christian thought. He was chiefly concerned with the branch of philosophy known as ontology (the study of being) and described God as the "ground of being."

Trump, Donald (b. 1946). American billionaire real-estate developer.

Wagner, Richard (1813–1883). German composer of operas and other works. His *The Ring of the Nibelung* (*Der Ring des Nibelungen*), commonly known as *The Ring Cycle*, is his best-known work.

Weinberg, Steven (b. 1933). American physicist. He won the Nobel Prize in Physics in 1979.

Wells, H. G. (1866–1946). English author of science fiction and social commentary.

Resources

Dostoyevsky, Fyodor. *The Brothers Karamazov.* Translated by C. Garnett. Foreword by M. Komroff. New York: New American Library, Signet Classics, 1957.

———. *Crime and Punishment.* Translated by C. Garnett. Introduction by E. Simmons. New York: Modern Library, 1950.

Encyclopaedia Britannica, 15th ed. *Propaedia,* s.v. "The Cosmic Orphan," by Loren Eiseley.

*Kaufmann, Walter, ed. *Existentialism from Dostoyevsky to Sartre.* 2nd ed. New York: New American Library, Meridian, 1975.

MacLeish, Archibald. "The End of the World." In *Major American Poets*, p. 436. Ed. Oscar Williams and Edwin Long. New York: New American Library, 1962.

Morris, Thomas V. *Making Sense of It All: Pascal and the Meaning of Life.* Grand Rapids, Mich.: Eerdmans, 1992.

Pascal, Blaise. *Pensées.* Edited by Louis Lafuma. Translated by John Warrington. Everyman's Library. London: Dent, 1960.

Schaeffer, Francis. *Escape from Reason.* Downers Grove, Ill.: InterVarsity, 1968.

———. *The God Who Is There.* Downer's Grove, Ill.: InterVarsity, 1968.

* Advanced reading material

CHAPTER 3

WHY DOES ANYTHING AT ALL EXIST?

In the beginning was the Word, and the Word was with God, and the Word was God... All things came into being through him, and without him not one thing came into being. (John 1:1, 3 NRSV)

Before You Read Chapter Three

In this chapter Dr. Craig argues that God exists necessarily. What does it mean to say that God exists necessarily? A skeptic might say, "What do you mean, it's necessary for God to exist? That's just your opinion!"

In the philosophical sense that Dr. Craig is using the word, *necessarily* means that God cannot fail to exist. He exists in and of Himself and is not created or caused by anything else. The statement that God necessarily exists is an assertion of *how* the God that Christians believe in exists, not *that* the existence of God is closed to debate with skeptics.

This chapter introduces one of the major arguments for God's existence, the cosmological (from the Greek *kosmos* + *logia*, or study of the universe) argument. It states that the universe requires an ultimate ground of being or uncaused cause, which we identify as God. You have probably supported your belief in God by wondering why the universe exists. As you read this chapter, you'll gain a new appreciation of what a powerful reason you have to believe.

Chapter Summary

This chapter examines G. W. Leibniz's cosmological argument, which states that everything that exists has an explanation of its existence, either in the necessity of its own nature or in an external cause. Atheists counter that such a principle would require that God must have a cause to explain Him. But we can respond that the explanation of God's existence is that God exists by the necessity of His own nature, outside of space and time.

If atheists claim that the universe is an exception to the need for an explanation, they commit the taxicab fallacy (taking an argument only as far as you want it to go, instead of where it naturally leads). Nor can atheists beg the question by saying that the universe is all that there is, since that assumes that atheism is correct in asserting that the universe exists without God.

If the universe has an explanation of its existence, that explanation must be the unembodied and transcendent cause of space and time. The only candidate for such a being is God. At this point the atheist might try to backtrack and say that the universe exists by a necessity of its own nature, as Christians say that God does. However, the universe does not exist necessarily, since different sub-atomic particles could have existed. Given the existence of the universe, it therefore follows that the explanation of the universe's existence is God.

Reflection and Discussion

Reflection

Based on the information in this chapter, take some time to reflect on each of these questions prior to joining your group session.

- According to Leibniz, what is "the first question which should rightly be asked?"

- What are the two ways of explaining why something exists?

- Taking each of the chapter premises individually, summarize the supporting arguments offered for each of them. Refer to the chapter as necessary.

Discussion

Prior to meeting as a group, review the discussion questions below. You may even want to record your thoughts in a notebook. Be prepared to share your responses with the group. The group leader may choose to assign questions to specific group members or to simply read them aloud for open disucssion.

Clarify your understanding by reviewing the supporting arguments for the following premises:

> Presmise 1: Everything that exists has an explanation of its existence, either in the necessity of its own nature or in an external cause.

> Premise 2: If the universe has an explanation of its existence, that explanation is God.

> Premise 3: The universe exists.

For Further Discussion

If time permits, you may discuss these questions in your group, or consider them later during personal study.

- Why is the cause of the universe's existence not just some contrived Flying Spaghetti Monster as sarcastically suggested by some atheists?

- How should you respond to someone who says that appealing to God is not really giving an explanation, but only a pseudo-explanation masquerading as a real explanation?

Glossary

City College in Santa Barbara. A community college in Santa Barbara, California. Founded in 1909.

Keokuk. A city in the southeastern corner of Iowa, founded in the 1820s. Terminus of the Toledo, Peoria, & Western Railroad, a trans-Illinois line for which Dr. Craig's father worked.

Quarks. The smallest known elementary atomic particles. Quarks combine to form hadrons, which include protons and neutrons, the components of the atomic nucleus.

Taxicab Fallacy. The taxicab fallacy is committed if one fails to take an argument to its logical conclusion and instead only maintains the argument's premise until arriving at a predetermined conclusion. Hence, it is like taking a taxicab to where you have already decided to go.

University of Pittsburgh. University located in Pittsburgh, Pennsylvania. Founded in 1787.

Biographical Sketches

Grünbaum, Adolf (b. 1923). German-born philosopher of science at the University of Pittsburgh.

Leibniz, Gottfried Wilhelm (1646–1716). German philosopher, mathematician, and theologian. He is universally regarded as one of the great geniuses of world history. His many innovations include binary mathematics.

Schopenhauer, Arthur (1788–1860). German philosopher. He is known for his pessimistic atheism and his assertion that human desire cannot be completely fulfilled. He influenced later atheists including Nietzsche and Freud.

Resources

Craig, William Lane. *Reasonable Faith*, 3rd ed. rev., chap. 3. Wheaton, Ill.: Crossway, 2008.

Davis, Stephen T. "The Cosmological Argument and the Epistemic Status of Belief in God." *Philosophia Christi* 1 (1999): 5–15.

*————. *God, Reason, and Theistic Proofs*. Reason and Religion. Grand Rapids: Wm. B. Eerdmans, 1997.

Leibniz, G. W. F. von. "On the Ultimate Origin of Things." In *Leibniz Selections*, pp. 345–55. Ed. P. Wiener. New York: Scribner's, 1951.

————. "The Principles of Nature and of Grace, Based on Reason." In *Leibniz Selections*, pp. 522–33. Ed. P. Wiener. New York: Scribner's, 1951.

*O'Connor, Timothy. *Theism and Ultimate Explanation: The Necessary Shape of Contingency*. Oxford: Blackwell, 2008.

*Pruss, Alexander. "The Leibnizian Cosmological Argument." In *The Blackwell Companion to Natural Theology*, pp. 24-100. Ed. Wm. L. Craig and J. P. Moreland. Oxford: Wiley-Blackwell, 2009.

*————. *The Principle of Sufficient Reason: A Reassessment*. Cambridge Studies in Philosophy. Cambridge: Cambridge University Press, 2006.

*Advanced reading material

CHAPTER 4

WHY DID THE UNIVERSE BEGIN?

The heavens are telling the glory of God, and the firmament
proclaims his handiwork. (Psalm 19:1 RSV)

Before You Read Chapter Four

Some may consider a twelfth century Muslim theologian like al-Ghazali an unlikely source of inspiration for modern Christians. While we want to maintain the distinctive truths of Christianity, we can learn from non-Christians who have contemplated the question of God's existence. With his doctoral thesis in philosophy, Dr. Craig is known for reviving al-Ghazali's *kalam* cosmological argument. This deceptively simple argument establishes the fact that the universe had a beginning, and therefore the universe requires a cause.

That the universe had a beginning is something that you may take for granted, but atheistic philosophers have traditionally claimed that the universe is eternal in order to avoid the need for a creator.

Where does God come from? This is a popular question posed by atheists suggesting that it is better to imagine that matter has always existed rather than to believe that an eternal mind chose to create time, space, and the universe. Dr. Craig addresses this question in detail by showing both the acute philosophical difficulties in the idea of an infinite past as well as the scientific evidence for the absolute beginning of the universe.

Chapter Summary

The *kalam* cosmological argument states that whatever begins to exist has a cause. We know intuitively that something cannot come from nothing, despite some erroneous claims that physics gives examples of things coming from nothing. (There are *phase transitions* from one state of matter to the other, but no new matter is created.) Even true vacuums are not nothing. If something could come from nothing, then anything could come from nothing.

Philosophical argument and scientific evidence support the fact that the universe began to exist. If an actually infinite number of things cannot exist, there cannot have been an infinite number of past events. The use of actual infinites in mathematics does not avoid the issue, since mathematical theories establish only a universe of discourse. The existence of an imagined mathematical infinite in the real world doesn't make sense, as illustrated by Hilbert's Hotel and other examples.

Even if an actually infinite collection of things could exist, it could not have been formed by adding one member after another, which is the way the series of past events has been formed. Though some may argue that from any past point we can reach the present, inferring that the whole past could therefore have been crossed commits the fallacy of composition (falsely assuming that what is true of part of something is also true of the whole thing).

The expansion of the universe points to its having a beginning, despite the existence of non-standard models of the universe. These non-standard models, if viable, predict a beginning as well.

The thermodynamics of the universe and the process of entropy increase also show that the universe had a beginning. Attempts to find an alternate model of the universe have failed to avoid a beginning.

The universe must therefore have a cause. If the universe caused itself, it would have to exist *before* it came to exist. Therefore, the universe must have a transcendent cause—an uncaused, timeless, spaceless, immaterial, powerful, personal Creator.

Reflection and Discussion

Reflection

Based on the information in this chapter, take some time to reflect on each of these questions prior to joining your group session.

- Did the information in the chapter modify your understanding of what *nothing* truly means? Why is the statement "The universe tunneled into being out of nothing" misleading?

- Why isn't the universe an exception to the need for a cause?

- Though actually infinite sets are used in mathematics, they cannot exist in reality. What are some of the problems encountered when you attempt to create a physical model of an infinite set?

- Why is it not special pleading to say that God is eternal and uncaused?

- How is the idea of an infinite past absurd? Are you able to explain al-Ghazali's objections to an infinite past?

- How does the expansion of the universe show that the universe has a finite past?

- How does the second law of thermodynamics show that the universe has a finite past?

Discussion

Several potential objections to the *kalam* cosmological argument are covered in this chapter. Prior to meeting as a group, review the objections below. You may even want to record your thoughts in a notebook. Be prepared to share your responses with the group. The group leader may choose to assign questions to specific group members or to simply read them aloud for open disucssion.

- "Sub-atomic particles (so-called "virtual particles") come into being from nothing."

- "The universe tunneled into being out of nothing."

- "'Whatever begins to exist has a cause' is true of everything in the universe but not of the universe."

- "If everything has a cause, what is God's cause?"

- "According to modern set theory, the set of the natural numbers is actually infinite. So, contrary to al-Ghazali, an actually infinite number of things can exist."

- "In the Hilbert's Hotel illustration the absurdities result because the concept of infinity is beyond us and we can't understand it."

- "Even in a beginningless past, every event in the past is only a finite distance from the present."

For Further Discussion

If time permits, you may discuss these questions in your group, or consider them later during personal study.

- How did Einstein's theory of gravity lead to the Big Bang theory of the origin of the universe?

- What discovery by Edwin Hubble proved the universe was expanding?

- How is the expansion of the universe *not* like an explosion?

- Why is there is no center to the universe?

- Why can't the initial singularity itself be the ultimate cause?

- "Unless energy is being fed into a system, that system will become increasingly disorderly" is a statement of what principle?

* Why have contemporary physicists rejected Boltzmann's many worlds hypothesis?

* What is the problem with oscillating models of the universe?

* Who lost the bet between John Preskill and Stephen Hawking? Why?

* What is the problem with the self-caused universe proposed by Daniel Dennett?

Glossary

Actual Infinite. A collection which has more members than any natural number 1, 2, 3 . . . In mathematics, *actual* means *complete* and does not suggest that the set physically exists.

Bubble Universes. A proposed model within Chaotic Inflation theory that different regions of a multiverse have decayed to a true vacuum state at various times in cosmological history.

Entropy. In thermodynamics, the increase of irreversible changes in a system. Broadly, a measure of disorder within a system relative to the random ways that system may be arranged.

Fallacy of Composition. The logical fallacy of inferring that because something is true of a part of a thing it is also true of the whole.

General Theory of Relativity. The geometric theory of gravitation devised by Albert Einstein, which describes gravity as a property of spacetime. It is the basis of modern cosmology.

Second Law of Thermodynamics. A law of physics which states that entropy of an isolated system which is not in equilibrium will tend to increase over time. Entropy is the increase of irreversible changes in a system.

Thermodynamics. (Greek *therme dynamis*, "heat power") A field of physics that examines energy conversion between heat and mechanical work, and system variables such as temperature, volume, and pressure.

Metaphysics. (Greek *meta physika*, "beyond physical") A branch of philosophy that investigates the fundamental nature of reality.

Virtual Particles. A sub-atomic particle that exists for a limited time and space too small to measure. Virtual particles rely on the interaction of the fundamental forces of nature (electromagnetism, gravitation, strong nuclear force, and weak nuclear force) for their existence.

Wormholes. A hypothetical concept in physics that arises in general relativity, though there is no observational evidence of their existence. The wormhole is depicted as a "tunnel" though space and time.

University of Birmingham. University in Birmingham, England. It was chartered in 1900. Dr. Craig earned his Ph.D. in philosophy there in 1977.

Biographical Sketches

al-Ghazālī, Abū Hāmid Muhammad ibn Muhammad (1058-1111). Islamic theologian and philosopher. During the middle ages, his ideas influenced secular European thought as well as the Christian theologian Thomas Aquinas and the Jewish theologian Maimonides.

Boltzmann, Ludwig (1844–1906). Austrian physicist. He made early contributions to the field of thermodynamics.

Borde, Arvind (b. 1955). Professor of Mathematics at C.W. Post Campus of Long Island University.

Dennett, Daniel (b. 1942). Professor of Philosophy at Tufts University. An atheist, Dennett is known for ideas in the philosophy of biology, especially as they relate to biological evolution.

Einstein, Albert (1879–1955). Theoretical physicist and recipient of the Nobel Prize in Physics in 1921. He introduced the special and general theories of relativity, among many other innovations, which led to his recognition as the founder of modern physics.

Friedman, Alexander (1888–1925). Russian cosmologist and mathematician.

Guth, Alan (b. 1947). Theoretical physicist and cosmologist. He is a professor of Physics at the Massachusetts Institute of Technology and originated the inflationary universe theory.

Hawking, Stephen (b. 1942). Retired professor of theoretical physics at the University of Cambridge. He is known for his contributions to the understanding of cosmological black holes. Hawking is the recipient of multiple awards in his native England and the Presidential Medal of Freedom in the United States.

Hick, John (b. 1922). Philosopher of religion and theologian. He has held positions at the University of Birmingham, among other universities, and is the author of *Christianity at the Centre* and *The Myth of God Incarnate*. Hick has been reproached by conservative theologians for his theological pluralism.

Hilbert, David (1862–1943). German mathematician. He is known for the concept of Hilbert spaces, which are used in functional analysis.

Hubble, Edwin (1889–1953). American astronomer. He demonstrated the existence of galaxies other than the Milky Way and is the namesake of the Hubble Space Telescope.

LeMaître, Georges (1894–1966). Professor of physics and astronomer at the Catholic University of Leuven. He was an ordained priest and his hypothesis of the primeval atom helped lead to what became known as the Big Bang theory.

Preskill, John (b. 1953). American theoretical physicist and professor at the California Institute of Technology.

Smith, Quentin (b. 1952). American philosopher and professor of philosophy at Western Michigan University. Dr. Craig and Dr. Smith are personal friends and have debated multiple times and co-edited two books.

Vilenkin, Alexander. Professor of Physics and Cosmology at Tufts University. Pioneer of ideas of eternal inflation and quantum creation.

Resources

al-Ghāzalī. *Tahafut al-Falasifah* [*Incoherence of the Philosophers*]. Translated by Sabih Ahmad Kamali. Lahore, Pakistan: Pakistan Philosophical Congress, 1958.

*Craig, William Lane. *The Kalam Cosmological Argument*. Rep. ed. Eugene, Ore.: Wipf & Stock, 2001.

———. *Reasonable Faith,* 3rd ed. rev., chap. 3. Wheaton, Ill.: Crossway, 2008.

*Craig, William Lane and Antony Flew. *Does God Exist?* Ed. Stan Wallace. With responses by K. Yandell, P. Moser, D. Geivett, M. Martin, D. Yandell, W. Rowe, K. Parsons, and Wm. Wainwright. Aldershot, England: Ashgate, 2003.

*Craig, William Lane and James Sinclair. "The *Kalam* Cosmological Argument." In *The Blackwell Companion to Natural Theology*, pp. 101-201. Ed. Wm. L. Craig and J. P. Moreland. Oxford: Wiley-Blackwell, 2009.

Craig, William Lane and Walter Sinnott-Armstrong. *God?: A Debate between a Christian and an Atheist*. New York: Oxford University Press, 2003.

*Nowacki, Mark. *The Kalam Cosmological Argument for God*. Studies in Analytic Philosophy. Amherst, N.Y.: Prometheus Books, 2007.

*Oderberg, David. "Traversal of the Infinite, the 'Big Bang,' and the *Kalam* Cosmological Argument." *Philosophia Christi* 4 (2002): 303-34.

*Advanced reading material

CHAPTER 5

WHY IS THE UNIVERSE FINE-TUNED FOR LIFE?

Ever since the creation of the world his invisible nature, namely, his eternal power and deity, has been clearly perceived in the things that have been made. (Romans 1:20 RSV)

Before You Read Chapter Five

If people are asked why they believe in God, they frequently point to the design and beauty of the natural world. Skeptics might scoff at this response as overly simplistic. But recent advances in physics and cosmology show us how incredibly profound the design of the universe is and how carefully staged it is for human life. Renowned physicist Freeman Dyson, writing in his *Disturbing the Universe*, agreed that the universe is constructed in a manner hospitable to intelligent life. He summarized his position with the oft-quoted remark, "In some sense the universe knew we were coming."

Formally, the argument from design is called the teleological argument (Greek *telos*, "end" or "purpose"). Christians will find some of the strongest evidence for God's existence through studying the universe.

Chapter Summary

The fine-tuning of the universe for life is a scientific fact to be explained as a result of either physical necessity, chance, or design.

We can rule out physical necessity, since nature's fundamental constants and quantities are independent of nature's laws. Scientists are looking for a so-called "theory of everything," but such a theory, even if successful, will fall far short of explaining the fine-tuning of the universe.

Chance is no more successful an explanation, since the odds against a life-permitting universe are too great to be reasonably faced—unless one postulates the existence of an infinite, randomly ordered, world ensemble of universes. The many worlds hypothesis is a popular effort to avoid a designed universe, but such a "multiverse" may itself still require fine-tuning. Moreover, there are good reasons to reject the many worlds hypothesis. Not only do we have no evidence of the existence of so extravagant and contrived a hypothesis, but if such a multiverse existed, then we should be observing a very different universe than the one we do, in fact, observe.

Therefore, the fine-tuning is best explained by design. The question "Who designed the designer?" is not an objection to the design hypothesis, since in order to recognize an explanation as the best, you don't need to have an explanation of the explanation. Moreover, contrary to the claim that God is not a simple being, God, as an unembodied mind, is incomparably simpler than the universe.

Reflection and Discussion

Reflection

Based on the information in this chapter, take some time to reflect on each of these questions prior to joining your group session.

- The idea that a complex and delicate balance of initial conditions had to exist in the Big Bang for the universe to be life-permitting is known as what?

- What are the four basic forces of nature?

- What would happen if nature's constants and quantities were given different values?

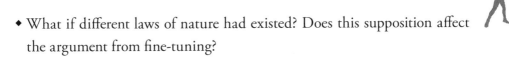

- What if different laws of nature had existed? Does this supposition affect the argument from fine-tuning?

- Does fine-tuning necessarily imply design?

- Dr. Craig states, "God is a remarkably simple entity." Why?

- What faith-based claim does Richard Dawkins make?

Discussion

Write a response to each of these skeptical statements mentioned in the chapter. Share your responses to the questions with your group. Discuss what you believe to be the flaws in their argument. The group leader may choose to assign questions to specific group members or to simply read them aloud for open disucssion.

- "But if the constants and quantities of nature had had different values, then maybe different forms of life might have evolved."

- "But maybe in a universe governed by different laws of nature, the loss of chemistry, matter, and planets might not result."

- "The designer hypothesis immediately raises the larger problem of who designed the designer."

- "We should not give up hope of a better explanation arising in physics, like something as powerful as Darwinism is for biology."

For Further Discussion

If time permits, you may discuss these questions in your group, or consider them later during personal study. Explain the flaws in each of these arguments:

- God is more complex than the universe—and an explanation should be simpler than what it explains.

* The cause of the universe doesn't have to be personal.

* The designer of the universe doesn't have to be good.

Glossary

Anthropic Principle. The assertion that we should not be surprised that the observed properties of our universe are compatible with the emergence of human life, since if they weren't, we couldn't be here to be surprised about it.

Big Bang. A cosmological model which asserts that the universe began expanding from an extremely hot, dense state about 14 billion years ago and continues to expand.

Cosmology. A branch of astronomy that examines the origin, structure, and dynamics of the universe.

Many Worlds Hypothesis. A hypothesis, derived from the branch of physics known as quantum mechanics, which uses the idea of multiple parallel universes to resolve paradoxes in the way atomic particles behave. Critics have borrowed this idea to try to explain how the universe could be fine-tuned despite the incomprehensible odds against it.

M-Theory or *Super-string Theory.* Based on the string theory version of quantum mechanics, M-theory analyses the basic substance of the universe by postulating eleven dimensions.

Multiverse. The idea of multiple parallel universes, of which our universe is one.

Plato's Academy. The name of the area where the Greek philosopher Plato taught during the 4th century BC. The word "academy" became a synonym for "school" in the 16th century.

Theory of Everything. A unified theory of physics that would explain all of the fundamental interactions in the natural universe via a single force carried by a single particle.

Thermodynamic Disorder (Entropy). A measure of disorder, that is, the number of random arrangements in a system. The system in question can be anything from a simple physical reaction to the entire universe. Entropy (thermodynamic disorder) tends to increase over time, expending energy and causing irreversible changes in a system.

Biographical Sketches

Barrow, John (b. 1952). English cosmologist, theoretical physicist, and mathematician. A fellow of the Royal Society, he is currently a professor at the University of Cambridge.

Leslie, John Andrew (b. 1940). Canadian philosopher and Professor Emeritus of philosophy at Canada's University of Guelph.

Penrose, Roger (b. 1931). English mathematical physicist at the University of Oxford. Co-recipient, together with Stephen Hawking, of the 1988 Wolf Prize for physics.

Resources

Collins, Robin. "A Scientific Argument for the Existence of God: The Fine-Tuning Design Argument." In *Reason for the Hope Within*, pp. 47-75. Ed. Michael J. Murray. Grand Rapids, Mich.: Eerdmans, 1999.

*————. "The Teleological Argument." In *The Blackwell Companion to Natural Theology*, pp. 202-81. Ed. Wm. L. Craig and J. P. Moreland. Oxford: Wiley-Blackwell, 2009.

Craig, William Lane. *Reasonable Faith,* 3rd ed. rev., chap. 4. Wheaton, Ill.: Crossway, 2008.

————. "Richard Dawkins on Arguments for God." In *God Is Great, God Is Good*, pp. 13-31. Ed. Wm. L. Craig and Chad Meister. Downers Grove, Ill.: InterVarsity, 2009.

*Craig, William Lane and Antony Flew. *Does God Exist?* Ed. Stan Wallace. With responses by K. Yandell, P. Moser, D. Geivett, M. Martin, D. Yandell, W. Rowe, K. Parsons, and Wm. Wainwright. Aldershot, England: Ashgate, 2003.

Craig, William Lane and Walter Sinnott-Armstrong. *God?: A Debate between a Christian and an Atheist*. New York: Oxford University Press, 2003.

*Leslie, John. *Universes*. London: Routledge, 1989.

Rees, Martin. *Just Six Numbers*. New York: Basic Books, 2000.

*Penrose, Roger. *The Road to Reality*. New York: Alfred A. Knopf, 2005.

Vilenkin, Alex. *Many Worlds in One: The Search for Other Universes*. New York: Hill and Wang, 2006.

*Advanced reading material

CHAPTER 6

CAN WE BE GOOD WITHOUT GOD?

No one is good but God alone. (Mark 10:18 RSV)

Before You Read Chapter Six

In chapter two, the moral implications of life without God were discussed. We can carry this discussion further by arguing that objective moral values and duties exist, that they aren't based in human society, and that they require a foundation in God.

In this chapter, Dr. Craig presents what is known as the moral argument for the existence of God. It is often misunderstood, and Dr. Craig confronts those misunderstandings at the beginning of the chapter.

Probably the easiest way to explain the moral argument is to explain what it's not. It is *not* the assertion that one has to be religious or Christian to be morally good. Rather, it's the assertion that moral truth requires an adequate explanatory ground. There must be a standard that is not found in any human being, organization, or society, but in a transcendent being, who is God. Defining morality as a social construct doesn't offer us an objective foundation for morality. The point of this argument is to show that a morally perfect being must exist to ground objective moral values and duties. The aim is not to convince the skeptic that unless he believes in such a being he is a bad person.

Chapter Summary

The moral argument for the existence of God is frequently misunderstood. It does not claim that atheists are necessarily bad people, or that one must be religious to be virtuous. The issue is the *existence* of God, not *belief* in God.

If God does not exist, objective moral values and duties do not exist. For without God naturalism is true, and morality is illusory. In a godless natural world, we would have no more moral value and duties than other animals.

One of the most common objections to the first premise of the moral argument is the Euthyphro dilemma: Is something good because God wills it? Or does God will something because it is good? If you say that something is good because God wills it, then what is good becomes arbitrary. But if you say that God wills something because it is good, then what is good or bad is independent of God. The correct response is to point out that the Euthyphro dilemma is a false dilemma. A third option is to affirm that God's nature is the good, and God's will is a necessary expression of His nature.

Another objection is atheistic moral platonism: moral values exist on their own as self-existent ideas. We may respond by noting three problems with atheistic moral platonism: it is unintelligible, it provides no basis for moral duty, and it is fantastically improbable because there is no reason why the natural realm and the independent moral realm should fit hand in glove.

Finally, there is stubborn humanism: whatever contributes to human flourishing is good, and whatever detracts from it is bad. The problem with this view is that humanism represents an arbitrary and implausible stopping point in the search for moral explanations. Why, given naturalism, are human beings valuable and why do they have any duties at all?

The main objection to the moral argument's second premise *that objective moral values and duties do exist* is the socio-biological account of morality—our moral beliefs have been ingrained into us by evolution and social conditioning. But the socio-biological account, if used as a challenge to the truth of our moral beliefs, commits the genetic fallacy, and, if used as a challenge to the justification of our moral beliefs, assumes that atheism is true and is ultimately self-defeating.

Reflection and Discussion

Reflection

Based on the information in this chapter, reflect on each of these questions prior to joining your group session.

- ◆ It is not necessary to believe in God to lead a moral life, acknowledge moral obligations and duties, or formulate a system of ethics. But if moral obligations and duties actually exist, what is necessary?

- ◆ Distinguish between values and duties. Which would you describe as being good or bad?

- ◆ Distinguish between being objective and subjective.

- ◆ What is the problem with claiming that morality is relative to culture? Or that morality is the product of social conditioning?

- ◆ We acknowledge a different standard for humans than for animals, whose actions are without moral dimension. What makes human actions prohibited or obligatory?

- ◆ How have atheists used the Euthyphro dilemma in an attempt to undermine the moral argument for the existence of God?

- ◆ Plato's assertion that the Good is its own self-existent idea seems implausible. Why?

Discussion

Prior to meeting as a group, review the discussion questions below. You may even want to record your thoughts in a notebook. Be prepared to share your responses with the group. The group leader may choose to assign questions to specific group members or to simply read them aloud for open disucssion.

- If God is essential to moral truth, then how is it possible for the millions and millions of people who don't believe in God to behave morally and ethically?

- Is something good because God wills it? Or does God will something because it is good?

How would you respond to each of the following assertions?

- "Moral values like justice, mercy, love, just exist without any foundation."

- "Whatever contributes to human flourishing is good, and whatever detracts from it is bad."

- "Our moral beliefs have been ingrained into us by evolution and social conditioning."

For Further Discussion

If time permits, you may discuss these questions in your group, or consider them later during personal study.

- Is it necessary to believe in God for one to be bound by objective morality?

Glossary

Relativism. A school of philosophy that rejects absolute truths. Moral relativism, for example, rejects absolute moral truths, insisting that morals are determined by social or cultural circumstances.

Sophie's Choice. The dilemma of being forced to choose between several options, which will all produce bad outcomes. It is named for the title character in William Styron's 1979 novel, *Sophie's Choice*, who faces such a dilemma.

Homo Sapiens. The species name for human beings in biological classification. *Homo* is Latin for "man" and "sapiens" means "wise" or "knowing".

Euthyphro Dilemma. A dilemma proposed in Plato's *Euthyphro* where Socrates and Euthyphro attempt to define moral goodness. The dilemma may be stated as: Does God will something because it is good, or is it good because God wills it?

Straw Man. In a debate, someone attacks a straw man when he misrepresents his opponent's position and proceeds to refute the misrepresented version, rather than the opponent's actual position. Just as scarecrow isn't a real person, a straw man argument isn't what the debate opponent actually believes.

Biographical Sketches

Adams, Robert (b. 1937). American philosopher. Currently affiliated with the University of North Carolina at Chapel Hill, Adams has held past positions at Yale, Oxford, and the University of California at Los Angeles.

Alston, William (1921–2009). Professor of philosophy at Syracuse University. An influential analytic philosopher, he made contributions to many topics of philosophy and was a founding member of the Society of Christian Philosophers.

Antony, Louise. Professor of philosophy at the University of Massachusetts at Amherst. She is the co-editor of *A Mind of One's Own*. Antony believes Western philosophy values reason and objectivity due to the bias of the white males who formulated philosophy in the Western world. Dr. Craig debated her in 2008 on the question, "Is God Necessary for Morality?"

Kurtz, Paul (b. 1925). Professor Emeritus of Philosophy at the State University of New York at Buffalo. As an influential secular humanist, he founded the Committee for Skeptical Inquiry in 1976. Dr. Craig's debate with Professor Kurtz at Franklin and Marshall College formed the basis for the book *Is Goodness without God Good Enough?*

Quinn, Philip (1940–2004). Philosopher of science and religion. He held positions at Brown University and the University of Notre Dame.

Sinnott-Armstrong, Walter (b. 1955). Professor of Philosophy at Dartmouth University. Two of his debates with Dr. Craig formed the basis for the book *God?: A Debate between a Christian and an Atheist*.

Sorley, William (1855–1935). Professor of Philosophy at the University of Cambridge.

Resources

*Alston, William. "What Euthyphro Should Have Said." In *Philosophy of Religion: A Reader and Guide*, pp. 283-98. Ed. Wm. L. Craig. New Brunswick, N. J.: Rutgers University Press, 2002.

Copan, Paul. "God, Naturalism, and the Foundations of Morality." In *The Future of Atheism: Alister McGrath and Daniel Dennett in Dialogue.* Ed. R. Stewart. Minneapolis: Fortress Press, 2008.

Craig, William Lane. *Reasonable Faith,* 3rd ed. rev., chap. 3. Wheaton, Ill.: Crossway, 2008.

———. "Richard Dawkins on Arguments for God." In *God Is Great, God Is Good*, pp. 13-31. Ed. Wm. L Craig and Chad Meister. Downers Grove, Ill.: InterVarsity, 2009.

*Craig, William Lane and Antony Flew. *Does God Exist?* Ed. Stan Wallace. With responses by K. Yandell, P. Moser, D. Geivett, M. Martin, D. Yandell, W. Rowe, K. Parsons, and Wm. Wainwright. Aldershot, England: Ashgate, 2003.

*Craig, William Lane and Paul Kurtz. *Is Goodness without God Good Enough?* Ed. Nathan King and Robert Garcia. With responses by Louise Antony, Walter Sinnott-Armstrong, John Hare, Donald Hubin, Stephen Layman, Mark Murphy, and Richard Swinburne. Lanham, Md.: Rowman & Littlefield, 2008.

Craig, William Lane and Walter Sinnott-Armstrong. *God?: A Debate between a Christian and an Atheist.* New York: Oxford University Press, 2003.

*Linville, Mark. "The Moral Argument." In *The Blackwell Companion to Natural Theology*, pp. 391-48. Ed. Wm. L. Craig and J. P. Moreland. Oxford: Wiley-Blackwell, 2009.

*Quinn, Philip L. *Divine Commands and Moral Requirements*. Oxford: Clarendon Press, 1978.

Ruse, Michael. "Evolutionary Theory and Christian Ethics." In *The Darwinian Paradigm*, pp. 262–69. London: Routledge, 1989.

*Sorley, William R. *Moral Values and the Idea of God*. New York: Macmillan, 1930.

*Advanced reading material

CHAPTER 7

WHAT ABOUT SUFFERING?

We also rejoice in our sufferings, because we know that suffering produces perseverance; perseverance, character; and character, hope. (Romans 5:3-4 NIV)

Before You Read Chapter Seven

One of the most common arguments used against believers, since the days of the ancient Greeks, is known as the problem of evil or the argument from suffering. It argues on the basis of the evil in the world against the existence of God as an all-good and all-powerful being. This underscores the importance of what we've learned in previous chapters. Given the previously cited arguments for the existence of God, the argument from suffering loses some of its force, but it is still a challenge for any Christian. For not only will atheists question our faith, but we may doubt faith ourselves when confronted with tragedy.

Christianity, however, doesn't hide from tragedy. Jesus suffered and died for us, and a great portion of Scripture recounts the tribulations of earthly life. We have a mission to contend with and confront evil, as well as ponder the questions it poses.

Think of an incident in your own life, of someone you know, or even a catastrophic event like those mentioned in this chapter, where you have questioned the love of God. Can you think of a specific question you had about God's attitude toward evil? Look for the possible answers as you read.

Chapter Summary

After dismissing several ineffectual arguments in support of atheism, Dr. Craig examines the argument from suffering, which he takes to be a more meaningful challenge. He distinguishes between intellectual and emotional versions of the problem. The intellectual version takes two forms: the logical version and the evidential version.

According to the logical version of the argument from suffering, the statements "God exists" and "suffering exists" are logically inconsistent. But we can answer the atheist by showing that no logical inconsistency has been proved between these statements; on the contrary, given the possibility of human freedom, it's plausible that they are wholly consistent.

The evidential version asserts that the statement "God exists" is improbable given the suffering in the world. A threefold response is given to this challenge. First, we are not in a position to judge that God lacks morally sufficient reasons for permitting the suffering in the world. Second, relative to the full scope of the evidence, God's existence is quite probable. And third, certain Christian doctrines increase the probability of the co-existence of God and suffering, so that the existence of the Christian God cannot be said to be improbable relative to the suffering in the world.

As for the emotional problem posed by suffering, many people adopt an atheism of rejection simply on emotional grounds. Here the Christian faith offers comfort and hope to those who are emotionally hurting. It reminds us that God, in the person of Jesus, was not exempt from suffering. He comforts and strengthens us amid the difficulties of a fallen world until we find eternal happiness in the afterlife.

Reflection and Discussion

Reflection

Based on the information in this chapter, take some time to reflect on each of these questions prior to joining your group session.

- Imagine that an atheist asks you, "If God is all powerful, could he create an object that is too heavy for him to lift?" Based on what you've learned in this chapter, how would you answer?

- Some people question whether it's plausible to think that God and suffering can co-exist, while others dislike a God who would permit suffering. Explain the distinction between these points of view.

- Christians often bear the burden of proof when arguing for the existence of God. Considering the problem of suffering, how would you explain to an atheist that he must shoulder the burden of proof when making this case against God?

- How is the existence of evil related to objective moral values?

Discussion

Prior to meeting as a group, review the discussion questions below. You may even want to record your thoughts in a notebook. Be prepared to share your responses with the group. The group leader may choose to assign questions to specific group members or to simply read them aloud for open disucssion.

- Why is the existence of suffering insufficient to rule out the existence of God? What should determine the probability of God's existence?

- Christianity uniquely addresses the problem of suffering in ways that other religions do not. How does Christianity respond to the evil in nature? In humanity? According to Scripture, what attitude should we adopt toward the suffering each of us must endure?

- God's being all-powerful does not mean that He can bring about the logically impossible, such making a square circle or *making* someone do something *freely*. Thus, human free will is often offered as defense against the problem from suffering. In responding to this, atheist Sam Harris has argued that our thoughts are the product of purely natural processes in our brain and, as such, free will is an illusion. What does this say about his own choice to be an atheist? If we assume that free will is an illusion, then how would we hold criminals accountable for murder, rape, or genocide? Would it be right to condemn someone for a choice that he did not freely make?

• In Genesis, when Adam and Eve obtain the knowledge of good and evil, they are cast out of paradise—the Garden of Eden. Their free will to obey or disobey God had serious consequences. Is God's gift of free will to mankind compatible with His love for us?

• It's not unusual to wish that you could live your life over again. But if you could start over, would you be able to make the proper free will choices to ensure your desired outcome? Assuming that bad things happened to you in this second life, would you be upset that God gave you free will?

• Christianity thrives under persecution as people rediscover the importance of God in their lives, so suffering may bring about positive ends. Compare that to hedonism—an ethical philosophy that says pleasure is our only goal in life—and its effect on individuals and societies. Can you think of any examples of hedonism's effects?

• If a skeptic told you that Christians ignore the suffering in the world because they are focused on an eventual heavenly reward, how would you respond?

For Further Discussion

If time permits, you may discuss these questions in your group, or consider them later during personal study.

◆ You may know people who have lost their faith due to tragedy, while others may seek God for the first time after a tragic event. How do you account for their opposite responses?

◆ Consider the story of Mabel at the end of the chapter. Do you know of someone who has persevered in the faith under similar circumstances? How do you think you would react under such trying conditions?

Glossary

Chaos Theory. A theory of how dynamical systems behave when small changes occur in the initial conditions of the system.

D-Day. June 6, 1944, when the Allied forces, led by the United States, launched their effort to liberate Europe from the Nazis.

Sliding Doors. 1998 film written and directed by Peter Howitt.

Wheaton College. A private Christian liberal arts college in Wheaton, Illinois. Dr. Craig is an alumnus of Wheaton College.

Biographical Sketches

Wolpert, Lewis (b. 1929). British developmental biologist and secular humanist. Dr. Craig debated him in Central Hall, Westminster, London.

Resources

*Adams, Marilyn McCord. *Horrendous Evils and the Goodness of God.* Ithaca, N.Y.: Cornell University Press, 1999.

Craig, William Lane. *Hard Questions, Real Answers.* Wheaton, Ill.: Crossway, 2003.

Craig, William Lane and J. P. Moreland. *Philosophical Foundations of a Christian Worldview,* chap. 27. Downer's Grove, Ill.: InterVarsity Press, 2003.

Craig, William Lane and Walter Sinnott-Armstrong. *God?: A Debate between a Christian and an Atheist.* New York: Oxford University Press, 2003.

*Howard-Snyder, Daniel, ed. *The Evidential Argument from Evil.* Bloomington, Ind.: Indiana University Press, 1996.

*Plantinga, Alvin. *God, Freedom, and Evil.* New York: Harper & Row, 1974.

*Van Inwagen, Peter. *The Problem of Evil.* Oxford University Press, 2006.

*Advanced reading material

CHAPTER 8

WHO WAS JESUS ?

And he asked them, "But who do you say that I am?" (Mark 8:29 RSV)

Before You Read Chapter Eight

The promise of eternal life was encapsulated in Christianity's defining event—Jesus' resurrection. Apart from a risen Christ, as Paul tells us in I Corinthians, our faith is in vain. So the Christian faith depends on two things about Jesus: that He is the Christ and that He has been raised from the dead.

Before we can examine the evidence for the resurrection, we need to establish the historical context, including exactly who Jesus claimed to be. If Jesus claimed to be the Anointed One, (*Messiah* in Hebrew, or *Christ* in Greek) of God, then we have a historical context that is fraught with religious significance.

In this chapter, Dr. Craig establishes who Jesus claimed to be, in preparation for an examination of the resurrection evidence presented in the following chapter.

Chapter Summary

Jesus produced two unique, unexpected beliefs about His person in His Jewish followers. First, they accepted Jesus as Messiah, even though He did not set up an earthly kingdom as the Messiah was expected to do. Second, they worshipped Jesus as God incarnate. Their understanding of monotheism would not easily accommodate worshipping a man as God in the flesh. Yet, that is exactly what they did within 20 years of His death. An adequate cause is required for these remarkable beliefs.

The explanation most plausibly lies in Jesus' own divine-human self-understanding and actions that affirmed His divinity. In this chapter, Dr. Craig probes the Gospels in order to discover Jesus' own self-understanding.

Since Jesus left no writing of His own, we are dependent on others for our knowledge of Jesus' unique claims about Himself. Contrary to radical critics, the New Testament documents are our primary source of information for the historical Jesus. The New Testament's earliest documents appear within the lifetime of eyewitnesses to Jesus' ministry. There was insufficient time for legendary influences to expunge the core historical facts, so the New Testament writings should not be presumed to be unreliable. Given the reliability of the Jewish transmission of sacred traditions, and corroboration by secular sources, the Gospels have a solid track record of historical reliability.

The Gospels traditions feature many positive signs of historical credibility, including fidelity to known historical facts, multiple early sources that don't rely on each other, details embarrassing to the early Christian church, dissimilarity to previous Jewish or later Christian ideas, traces of Hebrew and Aramaic spoken in Jesus' day, and coherence with other known facts about Jesus.

We can gain insight into Jesus' self-understanding through His explicit self-descriptions. Peter's acknowledgement of Jesus as Messiah, which Jesus accepts, and Jesus' reply to John the Baptist in prison are among the many evidences we have that Jesus saw Himself as Messiah. Though scholars typically see the Messiah as a human figure, the idea of a divine Messiah existed in Jesus' day, as evidenced by passages in Isaiah and the extra-biblical Similitudes of Enoch.

Jesus' parable of the wicked tenants of the vineyard tells us that He thought of Himself as God's only Son, distinct from all the prophets, God's final messenger, and the heir of Israel, pointing to a unique relationship as Son of God.

Jesus' favorite self-designation was the Son of Man. While some critics maintain that in calling Himself Son of Man Jesus merely meant "a human person," Jesus did not refer to Himself as "a son of man," but as "*the* Son of Man."

Jesus' consistent use of the phrase with the definite article "the" shows that He thought of Himself as the divine-human Son of Man predicted by the prophet Daniel.

Jesus also made implicit personal claims that reveal His self-understanding. In the content and style of His teaching, Jesus equated His own authority with that of the divinely given Law. He believed Himself to be not only an exorcist but a miracle worker. He expressed His authority by teaching in His own name, using the words "Truly, truly I say to you." Jesus' fellow Jews, as well as modern Judaism, would see this as unacceptably presumptuous behavior for a mere man. Jesus also held that people's attitudes toward Himself would be the determining factor in how God will judge them on the Judgment Day.

These examples clearly disclose the radical self-concept of Jesus. There is now virtually a consensus that Jesus claimed the authority to stand in God's place. These radical personal claims and activities led to His trial and crucifixion, facts unanimously accepted by historians. Through understanding Jesus' self-concept, we establish a proper historical context for evaluating the evidence for Jesus' resurrection.

Reflection and Discussion

Reflection

Based on the information in this chapter, take some time to reflect on each of these questions prior to joining your group session.

- ♦ Relative to other ancient historic figures, how much information do we have about Jesus?

- ♦ Was the New Testament written as a single, complete work? Why is it the *primary* source for information about the historical Jesus?

- ♦ If someone said, "The life of Jesus should be examined using unbiased sources outside of the New Testament," how would you respond?

♦ Is "Christ" a title or a proper name?

♦ Explain the legend hypothesis and why it is flawed.

♦ Give at least two examples supporting the historical reliability of the Gospels.

♦ Explain the difference between the *explicit* and *implicit* claims made by Jesus about His identity.

During your personal study you may want to review these scripture passages mentioned in the chapter.

♦ Peter's confession (Mark 8:27-30; John 6:69)

♦ Jesus' answer to John the Baptist (Luke 3:15-16; John 1:19-27)

♦ Jesus' triumphal entry (Mark 11:1-11; John 12:12-19; Zechariah 9:9)

♦ Jesus' action in the Temple (Matthew 21:12, 13; Luke 19:45, 46)

♦ Jesus' condemnation by the Sanhedrin (Matthew 26:59)

♦ Jesus' crucifixion as "King of the Jews" (Mark 15:26; John 19:19)

♦ The Son of God (Matthew 11:27)

♦ Parable of the Vineyard (Matthew 20:1-15)

♦ "No one knows the Father but the Son" (Matthew 11:27; Luke 10:22)

♦ "No one knows ... not even the Son" (Mark 13:32)

♦ Jesus' trial confession (Mark 14:26)

♦ "The Son of Man" referred to the divine-human figure of Daniel 7

♦ Jesus' preaching of the Kingdom of God (Luke 9:11-62)

♦ Jesus' authority (Matthew 7:28-29)

♦ Jesus' role as an exorcist (Luke 11:20)

- Jesus' claim to forgive sins (Mark 2:1-12)

- Jesus' role as Judge (Luke 12:8-9)

- Jesus' claim to forgive sins (Mark 2:1-12)

Discussion

This discussion time will be a bit different. Prior to meeting, take some time to review and record your answers for Part 2. Be prepared to share your thoughts with the group. You may find it helpful to familiarize yourself with the questions for Part 1. The group leader may choose to assign the Part 2 questions to specific group members or to simply read them aloud for open disucssion.

Part 1: Jesus' Explicit Claims

Divide your group into two teams. One team will play the skeptics and the other team the apologists. The skeptics will challenge the apologists with the statements listed below. A different representative from each team will participate for each of the different statements. Without referring back to the chapter, see how well each apologist can answer the skeptic. The skeptic should challenge the apologist with follow-up questions to draw as much information out of the apologist as possible. You may consider having the skeptics and apologists switch roles and repeat the exercise.

- "The historical Jesus never claimed to be the Messiah."

- "Jesus failed to do what was expected of the Messiah."

- "If Jesus had actually made a triumphal entry into Jerusalem, the Romans would have arrested Him immediately."

- "Jewish kings were referred to as God's sons, so Jesus' use of the title is not unique."

• "When Jesus said that He was 'a son of man', He merely meant that He was 'a human person.'"

Part 2: Jesus' Implicit Claims

Discuss the following questions as a group.

• Who will judge the twelve tribes of Israel? What does that imply about Jesus? Why?

• When Jesus says, "But I say to you…" and "Truly, truly I say to you" what is significant about His use of the pronoun "I" in the context of Jewish tradition?

• What is significant about Jesus' revising the Law of Moses in Matthew 5:31-32?

• Explain the significance Luke 11:20: "But if it is by the finger of God that I cast out demons, then the kingdom of God has come upon you."

• Name two ways in which Jesus' claim to forgive sins ran counter to Jewish thought.

• Jesus' contemporaries knew of Jewish holy men who performed wonders. What was different and unique about the miracles of Jesus?

• What, according to Jesus, determines how God will judge people on Judgment Day?

For Further Discussion

If time permits, you may discuss these questions in your group, or consider them later during personal study.

• The central figures of other world religions are very different from Jesus.

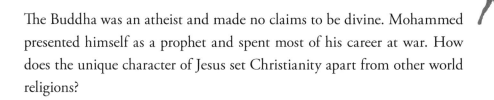

The Buddha was an atheist and made no claims to be divine. Mohammed presented himself as a prophet and spent most of his career at war. How does the unique character of Jesus set Christianity apart from other world religions?

Glossary

Alexandrian. Refers to the Egyptian coastal city of Alexandria, founded in the 4th century BC.

Annals of Tacitus. Writings of the Roman historian Tacitus (AD 56?–117?) documenting the reigns of Roman emperors.

Apocryphal Gospels. Various writings that appeared much later than the writings collected into the canon of the New Testament. *Apocrypha* is Greek for "hidden writings."

Dead Sea Scrolls. Ancient biblical scrolls that were found in a group of caves near the Dead Sea in the area known as Qumran. The document cited as "4Q521" refers to the manuscript 521, found in Qumran's cave 4, and is entitled "Messianic Apocalypse".

Jerusalem. The capital and largest city in Israel, founded nearly six thousand years ago.

Koran. The central text of the Islamic religion, sometimes transliterated as "Qur'an".

Philippi. A city in ancient Greece, established in 356 BC.

Samothrace. A Greek island in the Aegean Sea, settled since at least the sixth century BC.

Sermon on the Mount. The sermon given by Jesus in Matthew 5-7.

Thucydides' Peloponnesian War. A history of 5th century BC war between Sparta and Athens recorded by Greek historian Thucydides (460?– 395? BC).

Troas. An ancient city on the Aegean coast of Turkey.

Biographical Sketches

Hemer, Colin (d. 1987). British classicist who turned to the study of New Testament history.

Hick, John (b. 1922). Philosopher of religion and theologian. He has held positions at the University of Birmingham and is the author of *Christianity at the Centre* and *The Myth of God Incarnate*. Professor Hick was Dr. Craig's doctoral supervisor.

John the Baptist. Apocalyptic preacher and forerunner of Jesus.

Joseph Caiaphas. Roman-appointed Jewish high priest from AD 18–37.

King Arthur and the Knights of the Round Table. A legendary British king and the members of his court, though many historians are doubtful that they actually existed.

Pesch, Rudolf (b. 1936). Former Professor of New Testament at German universities in Frankfurt am Main and Freiburg. Since 1984, he has served on the Structure of the Academy for Faith and Form in Munich.

Plato (428–347 BC). Classical Greek philosopher. He was a student of the Greek philosopher Socrates.

Pontius Pilate. Prefect of the Roman province of Judaea from AD 26–36. An inscribed limestone tablet featuring Pilate's name was found by archaeologists in 1961 and was dated between AD 26–37.

Robin Hood. A character based on a variety of sources in English folklore. Beginning in the 15th century, writers of fiction used the character in plays and stories, adding new details with each generation. The modern depiction of Robin Hood is most indebted to Howard Pyle's novel for young readers, *The Merry Adventures of Robin Hood*.

Sherwin-White, A. N. (1911–1993). British Greco-Roman historian at St John's

College, Oxford.

Socrates (c. 469–399 BC). Greek philosopher. His teachings are known only through his appearance in Plato's dialogues.

Resources

*Collins, John J. *The Scepter and the Star: The Messiahs of the Dead Sea Scrolls and Other Ancient Literature*. Anchor Bible Reference Library. New York: Doubleday, 1995.

Craig, William Lane. *Reasonable Faith,* 3rd ed. rev., chap. 7. Wheaton, Ill.: Crossway, 2008.

Dictionary of Jesus and the Gospels. Edited by Joel B. Green, Scot McKnight, and I. Howard Marshall. Downers Grove, Ill.: InterVarsity, 1992.

*Dunn, James D. G. *Christianity in the Making*. Vol. 1: *Jesus Remembered*. Grand Rapids, Mich.: Eerdmans, 2003.

*Ellis, E. E. "Dating the New Testament." *New Testament Studies* 26 (1980): 487–502.

Evans, Craig A. "Authenticity Criteria in Life of Jesus Research." *Christian Scholar's Review* 19 (1989): 6–31.

———. *Fabricating Jesus*. Downers Grove, Ill.: InterVarsity, 2006.

*———. "Life-of-Jesus Research and the Eclipse of Mythology." *Theological Studies* 54 (1993): 3–36.

*Evans, Craig A. and Bruce Chilton, eds. *Authenticating the Activities of Jesus*. New Testament Tools and Studies 28/2. Leiden: E. J. Brill, 1999.

Green, Michael, ed. *The Truth of God Incarnate*. Grand Rapids, Mich.: Eerdmans, 1977.

Gruenler, Royce Gordon. *New Approaches to Jesus and the Gospels*. Grand Rapids, Mich.: Baker, 1982.

Hagner, Donald A. *The Jewish Reclamation of Jesus*. Grand Rapids, Mich.: Zondervan, 1984.

*Hemer, Colin. *The Book of Acts in the Setting of Hellenistic History*. Edited by Conrad H. Gempf. Wissenschaftliche Untersuchungen zum Neuen Testament 49. Tübingen: J. C. B. Mohr, 1989.

*Hengel, Martin. *The Son of God: The Origin of Christology and the History of Jewish-Hellenistic Religion*. Translated by John Bowden. Philadelphia: Fortress, 1976.

*Hurtado, Larry W. *Lord Jesus Christ: Devotion to Jesus in Earliest Christianity*. Grand Rapids, Mich.: Eerdmans, 2003.

*Meier, John P. *A Marginal Jew*. 4 vols. Anchor Bible Reference Library. New York: Doubleday, 1991, 1994, 2001.

Moreland, J. P. and Michael J. Wilkins, eds. *Jesus Under Fire*. Grand Rapids, Mich.: Zondervan, 1995.

*Moule, C. F. D. *The Origins of Christology*. Cambridge: Cambridge University Press, 1977.

*Sherwin-White, A. N. *Roman Society and Roman Law in the New Testament*. Oxford: Clarendon, 1963.

*Stein, Robert H. "The Criteria for Authenticity." In *Gospel Perspectives I*, edited by R. T. France and David Wenham, pp. 225–63. Sheffield, England: JSOT Press, 1980.

Strobel, Lee. *The Case for Christ*. Grand Rapids, Mich.: Zondervan, 1998.

*Twelftree, Graham H. *Jesus the Miracle Worker*. Downers Grove, Ill.: InterVarsity, 1999.

*Witherington III, Ben. *The Christology of Jesus*. Minneapolis: Fortress Press, 1990.

*Wright, N. T. *Christian Origins and the Question of God*. 3 vols. Minneapolis: Fortress Press, 1992, 1996, 2003.

*Advanced reading material

CHAPTER 9

DID JESUS RISE FROM THE DEAD?

Why seek ye the living among the dead? (Luke 24:5 KJV)

Before You Read Chapter Nine

When scholars refer to the *historicity* of ancient events, they mean that the events actually occurred, rather than are the product of fabrication or legend. The historicity of resurrection of Jesus is supported by multiple lines of evidence.

Our assurance of eternal life is based on Jesus' resurrection. Why do you think that Jesus, as a crucified and resurrected Savior, has appealed to more people throughout history than the central figures of other religions? In examining the reliability of the resurrection accounts in the gospels, Dr. Craig answers a wide array of skeptical challenges.

Chapter Summary

There are three facts that must be explained: the discovery of Jesus' empty tomb, the post-mortem appearances of Jesus, and the very origin of the Christian faith.

On the first day of the week following his crucifixion, Jesus' tomb was found empty by a group of His women followers. The historical reliability of the story of Jesus' burial, which is independently reported in very early sources, supports the historicity of the empty tomb. The testimony of women would not command the same respect as men's, and thus this detail is not what first century Jews would have used in a fictitious account. The account of the empty tomb in the oldest gospel, Mark, is simple and lacks signs of legendary development. Jesus' empty tomb is also presupposed in the earliest Jewish response to the disciples.

Various individuals and groups on different occasions and under varying circumstances experienced appearances of Jesus alive. Paul's list of eyewitnesses to Jesus' resurrection appearances in I Corinthians 15:3–5, which is a very ancient tradition, guarantees that such appearances occurred. The Gospel accounts provide multiple, independent reports of post-mortem appearances of Jesus, which were physical, bodily appearances.

The first disciples came sincerely to believe in Jesus' resurrection despite every predisposition to the contrary. Jews had no expectation of a Messiah who, instead triumphing over Israel's enemies, would be shamefully executed by them as a criminal. Jewish beliefs about the afterlife precluded anyone's rising from the dead to glory and immortality before the resurrection at the end of the world.

Explanations of these facts such as the conspiracy theory, the apparent death theory, the displaced body theory, and the hallucination theory do not fare well when assessed by the standard criteria for the best explanation. The best explanation includes its explanatory scope, explanatory power, plausibility, being contrived, disconfirmation by accepted beliefs, and the explanation's outstripping its rivals in meeting these criteria. The resurrection theory that God raised Jesus from the dead, when judged by the same criteria, emerges as the best explanation of the empty tomb, the post-mortem appearances, and the origin of the Christian faith.

Reflection and Discussion

Reflection

Based on the information in this chapter, take some time to reflect on each of these questions prior to joining your group session.

Think of at least two supporting arguments given in this chapter to establish each of these three facts of the resurrection. Refer back to the chapter as necessary.

- Jesus' empty tomb.

- Jesus' appearances after His death.

- The origin of the disciples' belief in His resurrection.

Which alternatives to the resurrection theory were represented by the following groups or individuals?

- 18th Century European Deists

- Early 19th Century Critics

- David Strauss (19th Century)

- Joseph Klausner (20th Century)

- Gerd Lüdemann (21st Century)

Identify the skeptical hypotheses represented by each of the following items. Without referring back to the chapter, recount the arguments given by skeptics about each hypothesis.

- Joseph of Arimathea moved the body

- The disciplines faked the resurrection

- Jesus wasn't dead after the crucifixion

- The resurrection appearances were hallucinations

Now, for each of the previous items, explain why the resurrection is a better explanation.

Discussion

Prior to meeting as a group, review the discussion questions below. You may even want to record your thoughts in a notebook. Be prepared to share your responses with the group. The group leader may choose to assign questions to specific group members or to simply read them aloud for open disucssion.

- What is the only new supposition required by the resurrection hypothesis? Does it seem like a contrivance?

- Most skeptics reject the idea of miracles altogether. How does establishing the historical context lend credibility to the miracle of the resurrection?

- Saul of Tarsus was a persecutor of Christians until an encounter with the risen Christ on the Damascus road spurred his transformation to Paul the Apostle. How does the uniqueness of Paul's experience lend credibility to the resurrection story?

- Beyond scriptural implications of a physical resurrection, what are other potential problems with explaining the resurrection on purely psychological grounds?

Divide your group into four equal teams. Each team chooses one of the alternate hypotheses to the resurrection—conspiracy, apparent death, displaced body, and hallucination theory. Within your team, compare the alternate hypothesis to the resurrection, determining which key points make the resurrection a better alternative. After ten minutes of discussion time, take turns sharing your analysis with the other teams.

Glossary

Achilles' Heel. A point of vulnerability. It refers to the mythological warrior Achilles, who appears in Homer's *Iliad*. According to the story, Achilles' mother dipped him in the river Styx while holding him by the heel. This action conferred immortality to every part of his body—except his heel.

Berachos 60b; Kiddushin 82b; Sotah 19a. Passages from the Talmud, an ancient collection of writings by Rabbis covering every aspect of Jewish law and tradition.

Biographical Sketches

Dodd, C. H. (1884–1973). British New Testament scholar and professor at the University of Cambridge.

Fuller, R. H. (1915–2007). Anglican priest and Bible scholar. He held professorial appointments throughout the English-speaking world, culminating his career as Professor Emeritus at Virginia Theological Seminary.

Grass, Hans. Late Professor at Philipps-Universität Marburg.

Habermas, Gary (b. 1950). Distinguished Professor of Apologetics and Philosophy at Liberty University. He is the chairman of the department of philosophy and theology at Liberty.

Josephus (AD 37–100?). First-century Jewish historian. His works are very valuable for developing an understanding of early Jewish and Christian history.

Klausner, Joseph (1874–1958). Lithuanian born Jewish scholar, specializing in Jewish religion, history, and Hebrew literature.

Lapide, Pinchas (1922–1997). Jewish theologian, historian, and Israeli diplomat.

Lüdemann, Gerd (b. 1946). Professor of History and Literature of Early Christianity at Georg-August-University in Göttingen, Germany.

Robinson, John A. T. (1919–1983). New Testament scholar and Dean of Trinity College. A theological liberal, he helped introduce secular theology.

Slezak, Peter (b. 1947). Professor at the University of New South Wales, Australia. He is a cognitive scientist, philosopher of science, and an atheist. Dr. Craig debated him before a packed house at the Town Hall in Sydney, Australia.

Stendahl, Krister (1921–2008). Swedish theologian and New Testament scholar and Professor Emeritus, Harvard Divinity School.

Strauss, David (1808–1874). German theologian and writer. He was a pioneer in the investigation of the historical Jesus and denied the divinity of Christ.

Vermes, Geza (b. 1924). Jewish religious historian. He is an authority on the Dead Sea Scrolls and has also written extensively about Jesus from a Jewish perspective.

Wright, N. T. (b. 1948). Bishop of Durham in the Church of England and New Testament scholar.

Resources

*Allison, Dale C., Jr. "Resurrecting Jesus." In *Resurrecting Jesus,* pp. 198–375. New York: T. & T. Clark, 2005.

*Alsup, John. *The Post-Resurrection Appearances of the Gospel Tradition.* Stuttgart: Calwer Verlag, 1975.

*Bode, Edward Lynn. *The First Easter Morning.* Analecta Biblica 45. Rome: Biblical Institute Press, 1970.

*Brown, Raymond E. *The Death of the Messiah.* 2 vols. Garden City, N.Y.: Doubleday, 1994.

*Craig, William Lane. *Assessing the New Testament Evidence for the Historicity of the Resurrection of Jesus,* 3rd ed. Studies in the Bible and Early Christianity 16. Lewiston, N.Y.: Edwin Mellen, 2002.

*———. "Dale Allison on Jesus' Empty Tomb, his Postmortem Appearances, and the Origin of the Disciples' Belief in his Resurrection." *Philosophia Christi* 10 (2008): 293-301.

———. *Reasonable Faith,* 3rd ed. rev., chap. 8. Wheaton, Ill.: Crossway, 2008.

———. *The Son Rises.* Rep. ed.: Eugene, Ore.: Wipf & Stock, 2001.

Craig, William Lane and John Dominic Crossan. *Will the Real Jesus Please Stand Up?* Ed. Paul Copan. With responses by Robert Miller, Craig Blomberg, Marcus Borg, and Ben Witherington III. Grand Rapids, Mich.: Baker Bookhouse, 1998.

Craig, William Lane and Bart Ehrman. "Is There Historical Evidence for the Resurrection of Jesus?" See: http://www.reasonablefaith.org/site/PageServer?pagename=debates_main

Craig, William Lane and Gerd Lüdemann. *Jesus' Resurrection: Fact or Figment?* Ed. Paul Copan and R. Tacelli. With responses by Stephen T. Davis, Michael Goulder, Robert H. Gundry, and Roy Hoover. Downer's Grove, Ill.: InterVarsity Press, 2000.

*Gundry, Robert. *Sōma in Biblical Theology*. Cambridge: Cambridge University Press, 1976.

*McGrew, Lydia and Timothy McGrew. "The Argument from Miracles." In *The Blackwell Companion to Natural Theology*, pp. 101-201. Ed. Wm. L. Craig and J. P. Moreland. Oxford: Wiley-Blackwell, 2009.

Stewart, Robert B., ed. *The Resurrection: The Crossan-Wright Dialogue*. Minneapolis: Augsburg Fortress, 2005.

*Wright, N. T. *Christian Origins and the Question of God*, vol. 3: *The Resurrection of the Son of God*. Minneapolis: Fortress Press, 2003.

*Advanced reading material

CHAPTER 10

IS JESUS THE ONLY WAY TO GOD?

There is salvation in no one else, for there is no other name under heaven given among men by which we must be saved. (Acts 4:12 RSV)

Before You Read Chapter Ten

Cultural elites are quick to blame religious convictions for conflicts that actually stem from ethnic prejudice or political animosity. Therefore, they consider distinct religious truths to be a societal hazard. Other skeptics may see belief in God as harmless, so long as the believer doesn't lay claim to any exclusive truths. This poses a challenge because the preceding chapters of *On Guard* have presented persuasive reasons for believing in the biblical God.

Dr. Craig concludes *On Guard* by refuting some of the common arguments given for religious pluralism, the idea that all religions are paths to God, and defending Christian particularism, the position that salvation is found in Christ alone.

Chapter Summary

While the religious pluralist claims that it is arrogant and immoral to say that only one religion is true, this is actually an *ad hominem* fallacy (arguing against the man rather than explaining why the position is false). Moreover, the religious pluralist does the same thing: he thinks he alone is right and so, by his own argument, is also arrogant and immoral.

When the religious pluralist insists that "Christian beliefs are false because people believe in the religion of their own culture," he commits the genetic fallacy (trying to invalidate a position by describing how a person came to believe it). Furthermore, the pluralist is in the same boat: his own view is likewise culturally influenced.

What is the problem with Christian particularism? It can't be just the doctrine of hell, for on the biblical view people freely separate themselves from God forever against His will.

The problem can't be that some people are uninformed or misinformed about Christ and so are judged unfairly. For according to the Bible they are judged on the basis of the information they have through God's general revelation in nature. Rather the problem concerns people who do not respond to general revelation but who *would* have responded to the Gospel if only they had heard it. Their condemnation seems to be the result of bad luck.

What is the logic of the problem? There's no demonstrable contradiction between the statements "God is all-powerful and all-loving" and "Some people never hear the Gospel and are lost." Given human free will, there's no guarantee that a world of universal, free salvation is feasible for God. And even if it were, a world of universal salvation might have overriding deficiencies that make it less preferable than a world in which some people freely reject God.

Indeed, we can show that these statements are consistent by adding a third statement, "Possibly God has arranged the world to have an optimal balance between saved and lost, and those who never hear the Gospel and are lost would not have accepted if they had heard it." Such a possibility can't be said to be improbable either, since a world so ordered by God would be empirically indistinguishable from a world where people's births were a matter of accident.

Reflection and Discussion

Reflection

Based on the information in this chapter, take some time to reflect on each of these questions prior to joining your group session.

- Imagine that someone made both of the following statements in a conversation with you. What beliefs do you think motivate them to say such things? How would you respond?

  "It's arrogant and immoral to believe that only Christianity is true."
  "You're only a Christian because you were born in a Christian culture."

- Explain the two major ways that the Expansion of Europe led people to question Christian particularism.

- According to Dr. Craig, what is the real problem raised by the religious diversity of mankind?

- Some people may charge that God is unjust because the punishment of hell does not fit the crime of sin. Explain Dr. Craig's two responses.

- According to Dr. Craig, why did God have to accept that some people would freely reject Him and His every effort to save them and be lost?

- Dr. Craig writes, "the benefits of Christ's atoning death can be applied to people without their conscious knowledge of Christ." What is still necessary to obtain salvation?

- Can we distinguish in advance between someone who would become culturally Christian and someone who would believe in Christ for salvation?

Discussion

Prior to meeting as a group, review the discussion questions below. You may even want to record your thoughts in a notebook. Be prepared to share your responses with the group. The group leader may choose to assign questions to specific group members or to simply read them aloud for open disucssion.

◆ Beyond the examples given in the chapter, what do you believe offends non-Christians about the assertion that Christianity is uniquely true (Particularism)?

◆ What role does personal understanding play in salvation? What must you believe to be saved? Do you think that God will judge our theological beliefs?

◆ If you accepted religious pluralism as fact, how would it affect your Christian faith?

◆ We decide whether we are saved or lost. How might this have affected, or not affected, God's decisions in creating mankind and ordering the world?

Final Wrap-Up

Recall the exercise from chapter one and find your original responses to the skeptics' statements that are reprinted below. Answer them again, comparing your original response to how well you are able to answer them now that you have completed *On Guard*.

◆ "I'm spiritual, not religious. Why should it matter whether there's a God or not?"

◆ "The sooner we get rid of this superstitious fantasy of some Big Daddy in the sky, the better. Then, science can take its proper place as the true savior of humanity."

- "Loving kindness is my religion. Just be good to others and don't worry whether there's a God."

- "If there really is a God, he doesn't care how much we suffer."

- "I used to go to church, but when I didn't get anything I prayed for, I realized that there wasn't any God listening."

- "How can you believe that this guy that lived two thousand years ago came back to life from the dead?! Do you expect anyone else to do that? It doesn't make any sense!"

- "Christians are ignorant, bigoted, fascists! They think their religion is the only one that's right!"

If it was still difficult to respond to some of the statements, try reading the relevant chapter again. Also, you can find additional resources at Dr. Craig's website, www.reasonablefaith.org.

Glossary

Argument ad Hominem. Latin for "argument against the man." Attacking the character of a person asserting a position rather than attacking his position.

Genetic Fallacy. Attempting to invalidate a position by criticizing the way in which a person came to believe it.

Biographical Sketches

Aquinas, Thomas (1225?–1274). Italian Roman Catholic priest, philosopher, and natural theologian. He is the namesake of Thomistic school of philosophy and theology and is revered as one of the greatest thinkers in world history.

Augustine of Hippo (354–430). Early and immensely influential Christian philosopher and theologian. Wrote *City of God* (early 5th century).

Columbus, Christopher (1451?–1506). Italian explorer who initiated the colonization of the western hemisphere.

Hick, John (b. 1922). Philosopher of religion and theologian, who has held positions at the University of Birmingham among many other universities. Author of *Christianity at the Centre* and *The Myth of God Incarnate*.

Magellan, Ferdinand (1480–1521). Portuguese explorer who led the first expedition around the world.

Polo, Marco (1254–1324). Italian trader and worldwide explorer.

Voltaire (1694–1778). Pen name of François-Marie Arouet, French Enlightenment writer, essayist, and philosopher. He was a deist, meaning that he believed God existed but denied any particular revelation of God.

Resources

Craig, William Lane. *Hard Questions, Real Answers*. Wheaton, Ill.: Crossway, 2003.

*————. "Is 'Craig's Contentious Suggestion' Really So Implausible?" *Faith and Philosophy* 22 (2005): 358-61.

*————. "Is Uncertainty a Sound Foundation for Religious Tolerance?" In *Religious Tolerance through Humility*, pp. 13-27. Ed. James Kraft and David Basinger. Aldershot, England: Ashgate, 2008.

*————. "Should Peter Go to the Mission Field?" *Faith and Philosophy* 10 (1993): 261-65.

*————. "Talbott's Universalism." *Religious Studies* 27 (1991): 297-308.

Craig, William Lane and J. P. Moreland. *Philosophical Foundations of a Christian Worldview*, chap. 31. Downer's Grove, Ill.: InterVarsity Press, 2003.

*_Faith and Philosophy_ 14 (1997): 277-320. See articles by Hick, Alston, Mavrodes, Plantinga, Van Inwagen, and Clark.

Geivett, Douglas. "Some Misgivings about Evangelical Inclusivism." In *Who Will Be Saved?* Edited by Paul R. House and Gregory A Thornbury. Wheaton, Ill.: Crossway, 2000.

*Kvanvig, Jonathan L. *The Problem of Hell*. Oxford: Oxford University Press, 1993.

Murray, Michael J. "Heaven and Hell." In *A Reason for the Hope Within*, pp. 287-317. Edited by Michael J. Murray. Grand Rapids, Mich.: Wm. B. Eerdmans, 1999.

Okholm, Dennis L. and Timothy R. Phillips, eds. *Four Views on Salvation in a Pluralistic World*. Grand Rapids, Mich.: Zondervan, 1996.

*Quinn, Philip L. and Kevin Meeker, eds. *The Philosophical Challenge of Religious Diversity.* Oxford: Oxford University Press, 2000.

*Van Inwagen, Peter. "Non Est Hick." In *God, Knowledge, and Mystery*, pp. 191-216. Ithaca, N.Y.: Cornell University Press, 1995.

*Advanced reading material

Notes

For more information and resources by Dr. William Lane Craig
and to learn about the ministries of Reasonable Faith,
please visit us at:

www.reasonablefaith.org